HANUKKAH
Sweets and Treats

By Ronne Randall

WINDMILL
BOOKS

New York

Published in 2013 by Windmill Books, An Imprint of Rosen Publishing
29 East 21st Street, New York, NY 10010

First Edition

Produced for Windmill by Ruby Tuesday Books Ltd
Editor for Ruby Tuesday Books Ltd: Mark J. Sachner
US Editor: Sara Antill
Designer: Trudi Webb and Emma Randall

Photo Credits:
Cover, 1, 3, 4–5, 6–7, 8–9, 10–11, 12–13, 14–15, 16–17, 18–19, 20–21, 22–23, 24–25, 26–27, 28–29, 30–31 © Shutterstock.

Library of Congress Cataloging-in-Publication Data

Randall, Ronne.
 Hanukkah sweets and treats / by Ronne Randall.
    p. cm. — (Holiday cooking for kids!)
 Includes index.
 ISBN 978-1-4488-8083-6 (library binding) — ISBN 978-1-4488-8130-7 (pbk.) — ISBN 978-1-4488-8136-9 (6-pack)
 1. Hanukkah cooking—Juvenile literature. I. Title.
 TX739.2.H35R36 2013
 641.5'68—dc23
                                          2012006773

Manufactured in the United States of America

CPSIA Compliance Information: Batch #B3S12WM: For Further Information contact Windmill Books, New York, New York at 1-866-478-0556

Contents

A Festival of Light, Food, and Fun

In the darkest part of winter, the gift of light can seem like a **miracle**. Hanukkah, also known as the Festival of Lights, celebrates a brightly burning miracle that happened more than 2,000 years ago. At that time, the Jews were ruled by the Syrian-Greeks, who tried to force them to abandon their religion. Led by a band of rebels called the **Maccabees**, the Jews fought back, and won! But when they went to rededicate their temple by lighting the holy lamp, there was only enough oil for one day. According to tradition, the oil miraculously lasted for eight days, which was enough time for them to get a fresh supply.

Today, Jews everywhere remember that miracle by celebrating Hanukkah (which means "rededication") for eight days, with brightly burning candles, blessings, games, gifts, and yummy food!

The recipes in this book will give you lots of ways to make your Hanukkah brighter, tastier, and sweeter!

Before you start cooking, check out all the tips and information on the following pages.

Before You Begin Cooking

Get Ready to Cook

- Wash your hands using soap and hot water. This will help to keep bacteria away from your food.
- Make sure the kitchen countertop and all your equipment is clean.
- Read the recipe carefully before you start cooking. If you don't understand a step, ask an adult to help you.
- Gather all the ingredients and equipment you will need.

Safety First!

It's very, very important to have an adult around whenever you do any of the following tasks in the kitchen:

1. Operating machinery or turning on kitchen appliances such as a mixer, food processor, blender, stovetop burners, or the oven.

2. Using sharp utensils, such as knives, can openers, or vegetable peelers.

3. Working with hot pots, pans, or cookie sheets.

Colander · Saucepan · Rolling pin · Knife · Sieve · Cutting board · Frying pan · Wooden spoon · Electric hand mixer · Oven mitt · Grater · Baking tray · Vegetable peeler · Cookie sheet · Cupcake pan · Spatula

You will need these kitchen utensils to make the recipes in this book.

Measuring Counts!

Measure your ingredients carefully. If you get a measurement wrong, it could affect how successful your dish turns out to be. Measuring cups and spoons are two of the most important pieces of equipment in a kitchen.

Measuring cup

Measuring Cups

Measuring cups are used to measure the volume, or amount, of liquid or dry ingredients. Measuring cups usually hold from 1 cup to 4 cups. If you have a 1-cup measuring cup, that should be fine for all the recipes in this book. Measuring cups have markings on them that show how many cups or parts of a cup you are measuring.

Measuring Spoons

Like measuring cups, measuring spoons are used to measure the volume of liquid or dry ingredients, only in smaller amounts. Measuring spoons come in sets with different spoons for teaspoons, tablespoons, and smaller parts.

Measuring spoons

Cooking Techniques

Here are some tasks that anyone who is following directions for cooking should be sure to understand.

Bringing to a boil

Heating a liquid or mixture in a saucepan on the stovetop until it is bubbling.

Simmering

First bringing a liquid or mixture to a boil, and then turning down the heat so it's just at or below the boiling point and the bubbling has nearly stopped.

Preheating

Heating the oven until it has reached the temperature required for the recipe.

All of these tasks require the use of heat, so you should be absolutely sure to have an adult around when you do them.

Luscious Latkes

The Hanukkah miracle was all about oil, so it is traditional to celebrate the miracle by eating foods fried in oil. The most popular Hanukkah treats by far are the fried potato pancakes called latkes. No Hanukkah celebration is complete without a platter of yummy, crispy potato latkes. This recipe is easy, but make sure an adult helps you with the peeling, grating, and frying.

Happy Hanukkah Eating

Potatoes are an excellent source of **vitamin** C, which helps prevent a disease called scurvy. It also helps keep skin and gums healthy, and may help protect against colds and flu. During the Alaskan gold rush in the 1890s, miners valued potatoes so highly they traded them for gold!

You will need – ingredients:

These quantities make 15 to 20 latkes

4 large potatoes

1 medium onion, peeled

2 large eggs

1 teaspoon salt

¼ teaspoon ground pepper

1 tablespoon all-purpose flour

½ teaspoon baking powder

Vegetable oil for frying

Sour cream and/or applesauce for serving
(see recipe for applesauce on pages 12–15)

You will need – equipment:

Vegetable peeler

Grater or food processor

Colander or strainer

Large bowl

Wooden spoon

Spatula

Frying pan deep enough to fry with about
1 inch (2.5 cm) of oil

Potholder or oven mitt for holding frying
pan handle

Paper towels

Step-by-Step:

Remember to ask an adult for help when you are using the vegetable peeler, the food processor, the knife, and the stove.

1. Peel the potatoes. As you peel them, place them in a bowl of cold water so they don't turn brown.

2. Grate the potatoes and onion or put them in the food processor and pulse until they are roughly chopped.

3. Drain the grated potato and onion mixture in the colander or strainer, and press down on it with the wooden spoon to get as much liquid out of it as possible.

4. Put the grated potato and onion mixture, along with all the other ingredients, in the large bowl, and stir well.

5. Pour 1 inch (2.5 cm) of oil into the pan.

Step-by-Step:

6. Heat the oil in the pan until it is very hot. Be sure an adult supervises all the following steps involving frying and turning the latkes.

7. For each latke, take ¼ cup of the potato mixture and drop into the hot oil. Flatten the latke slightly with the spatula so that it is about 3 inches (7.6 cm) in diameter.

8. After about 4–5 minutes, carefully turn the latkes over with the spatula, and fry for another 4–5 minutes. The latkes should be golden brown on both sides.

9. When the latkes are done, use the spatula to remove them from the pan.

10. Drain the latkes for a few minutes on paper towels.

11. Your latkes are ready to eat! Enjoy them with some sour cream and sweet and tangy applesauce. The recipe for the applesauce is on the next page!

Easy Applesauce

Latkes are delicious all by themselves or with a scoop of sour cream, but they're even better accompanied by sweet, tangy applesauce. You can buy applesauce in jars, but it's so easy to make your own and it tastes better, too. Sweet varieties like Red Delicious or Gala apples will make a sweeter sauce. Sauce made from Granny Smith or McIntosh apples will be more tangy. Try using a combination and let the flavor surprise you!

You will need – ingredients:

4 medium to large apples

¾ cup water

¼ cup sugar

½ teaspoon ground cinnamon

You will need – equipment:

Vegetable peeler

Knife

Saucepan

Wooden spoon

Medium mixing bowl

Fork or potato masher

Step-by-Step:

Remember to ask an adult for help when you are using the vegetable peeler, the knife, and the stove.

1. Peel and core the apples, and slice into pieces.

2. Put the apples in the saucepan, along with all the other ingredients.

3. Cook over medium heat, stirring occasionally, until the apples are soft—probably about 20 minutes.

4. Pour the apples into the mixing bowl to allow them to cool a little.

5. Mash with a fork or potato masher.

6. Serve with potato latkes for an unbeatable Hanukkah treat!

Happy Hanukkah Eating

Apples probably originated in western Asia thousands of years ago, and the apple tree was the first fruit tree to be planted and grown by people. So apples were almost certainly eaten by the Jews in the time of the Maccabees. Who knows, maybe they even ate applesauce!

Fudgy Gelt

For hundreds, or possibly thousands, of years people have given Hanukkah gifts of money. In **Yiddish**, a language used by European Jews, this money is called gelt. According to one legend, after their victory over the Syrian-Greeks, the Maccabees and their followers minted coins to celebrate their victory. These days, all kinds of gifts are exchanged at Hanukkah, and children are given chocolate money instead of real coins. Here's an easy recipe for making your own fudgy money. Just remember that it's for eating, not spending!

Happy Hanukkah Eating

Everyone knows that money, even Hanukkah gelt, doesn't grow on trees. But chocolate does! Cocoa beans, the main ingredient of all the chocolate we eat, are the seeds of the cacao tree, which grows in tropical rain forests.

Cocoa pods on a cacao tree

Cocoa beans inside a pod

You will need – ingredients:

3 cups semisweet chocolate chips

14-ounce (414-ml) can of sweetened condensed milk

1 teaspoon vanilla extract

Pinch of salt

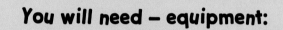

You will need – equipment:

Large bowl

Wooden spoon

Baking pan

Waxed paper

Bottle caps of various sizes

Aluminum foil

Gelt

Step-by-Step:

1. Put the chocolate chips and condensed milk in the bowl and heat in the microwave for 1–2 minutes. Stir until smooth. If the chocolate is not fully melted, heat it for another 10 seconds. Keep heating in 10-second bursts until fully melted.

2. Add the vanilla and salt, and stir until completely mixed.

3. Line the baking pan with the waxed paper, and pour the melted chocolate into the lined pan.

4. Refrigerate for a half hour, or until just firm.

5. Use the bottle caps to press coin shapes out of the fudge.

6. Wrap the coins in foil and use in the dreidel game or as party favors. Or just eat and enjoy!

Dreidel

NUN

SHIN

Happy Hanukkah Eating

The four-sided Hanukkah top called the dreidel has a Hebrew letter on each of its four sides. The letters— nun, gimel, hay, and shin—stand for the words "nes gadol haya sham," meaning "a great miracle happened there." You can use your fudgy gelt to play the dreidel game. Each player puts a piece of gelt into a pile, then takes a turn spinning the dreidel. If the nun is facing up when the dreidel stops, you get nothing. Gimel gives you everything in the pile. Hay gives you half, and if the dreidel lands on shin you have to put a coin in.

Delicious Donuts

Latkes are the most popular Hanukkah treat in the United States, but in Israel, Hanukkah makes most people think of *sufganiyot*, or donuts. The oil the donuts are fried in reminds us of the Hanukkah miracle, and their sweetness reminds us to have a sweet celebration.

Over the years sufganiyot have become more popular as a Hanukkah treat outside of Israel, and now you can make your own! If you want to make them without a jelly filling, just skip step 7. As always, ask an adult to help you with the frying.

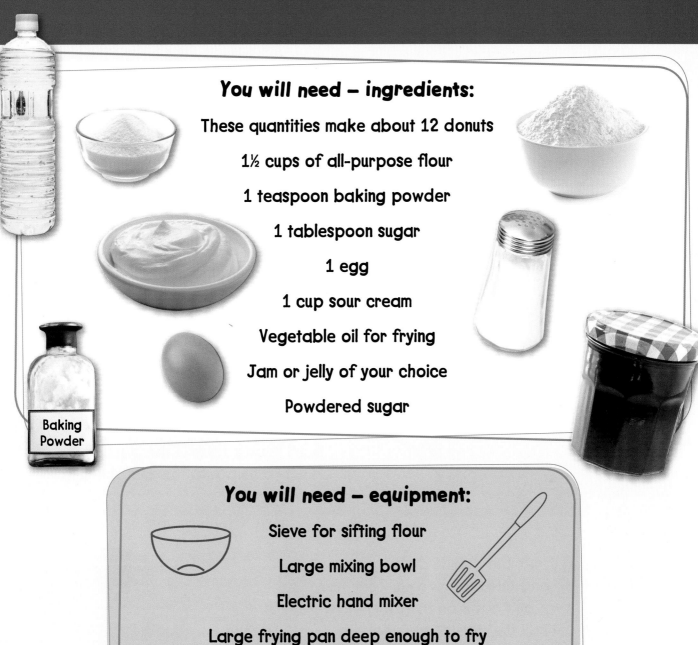

You will need – ingredients:

These quantities make about 12 donuts

1½ cups of all-purpose flour

1 teaspoon baking powder

1 tablespoon sugar

1 egg

1 cup sour cream

Vegetable oil for frying

Jam or jelly of your choice

Powdered sugar

Baking Powder

You will need – equipment:

Sieve for sifting flour

Large mixing bowl

Electric hand mixer

Large frying pan deep enough to fry
with about 2 inches (5 cm) of oil

Potholder or oven mitt for
holding frying pan handle

Paper towels

Spatula

Small spoon

Step-by-Step:

1. Sift the flour and baking powder into the large mixing bowl.

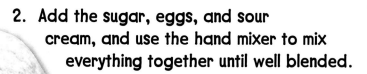

2. Add the sugar, eggs, and sour cream, and use the hand mixer to mix everything together until well blended.

3. Pour 2 inches (5 cm) of oil into the frying pan.

4. Heat the oil in the frying pan. When it is very hot, carefully add a tablespoon of batter for each donut to the oil. Don't crowd them in the pan! (Ask an adult to help with this and the next two steps.)

5. Fry until the donuts puff up and turn light brown. Then turn over and cook on the other side. Repeat until all the donuts are cooked.

6. Using a spatula, carefully remove the cooked donuts from the pan and place them on paper towels to absorb some of the oil, and to cool.

Remember to ask an adult for help when you are using the electric hand mixer and the hot frying pan and stove.

Step-by-Step:

7. When the donuts are cool, poke a small hole in each donut and carefully put in some jam or jelly, using a small spoon.

8. Sprinkle with powdered sugar and serve.

Happy Hanukkah Eating

Angel's Bakery, the largest bakery in Israel, produces up to 250,000 sufganiyot on each of the eight days of Hanukkah. They are fried in batches of 1,600 donuts each, and each batch uses about 220 pounds (100 kg) of **dough**. Think you could do that in your kitchen?

Hanukkah Cookies

Hanukkah treats don't have to be fried to be fun! These cute and tempting cookies will brighten up any Hanukkah celebration. Get your friends to help you decorate them, or surprise everyone with your own clever creations. They're sure to think you're one smart cookie!

Happy Hanukkah Eating

The six-pointed Star of David, or "Jewish star," has been used as a symbol on Jewish buildings, prayer books, and religious objects for more than a thousand years and has been the recognized emblem of the Jewish people since the 1600s. The colors blue and white are also associated with the Jewish people. They are the traditional colors of the *tallit*, the prayer shawl worn over the shoulders at Jewish Sabbath, holiday, and morning services.

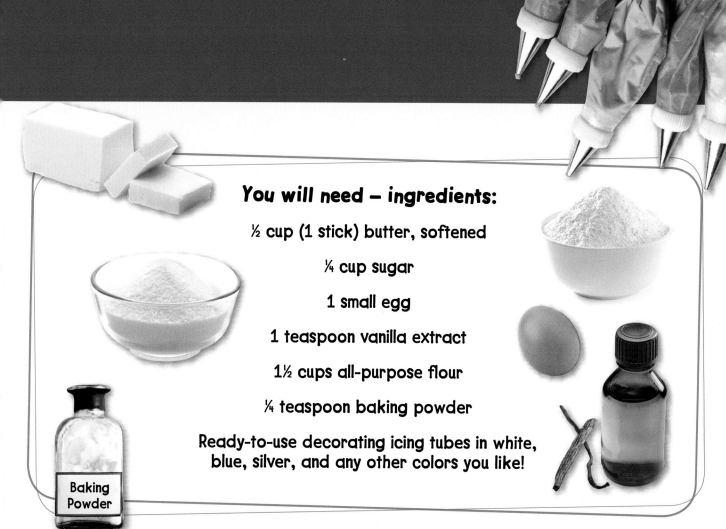

You will need – ingredients:

½ cup (1 stick) butter, softened

¼ cup sugar

1 small egg

1 teaspoon vanilla extract

1½ cups all-purpose flour

¼ teaspoon baking powder

Ready-to-use decorating icing tubes in white, blue, silver, and any other colors you like!

Baking Powder

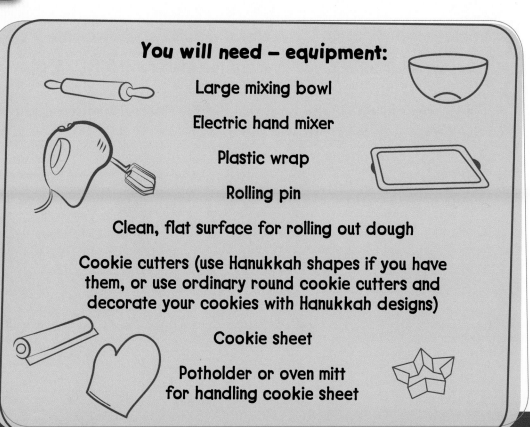

You will need – equipment:

Large mixing bowl

Electric hand mixer

Plastic wrap

Rolling pin

Clean, flat surface for rolling out dough

Cookie cutters (use Hanukkah shapes if you have them, or use ordinary round cookie cutters and decorate your cookies with Hanukkah designs)

Cookie sheet

Potholder or oven mitt for handling cookie sheet

Step-by-Step:

1. Using the electric mixer, beat the butter and sugar together until creamy, then add the egg and vanilla extract and beat until well blended.

2. Gradually add the flour and baking powder, and beat until it's just blended.

3. Shape the dough into a ball, wrap in plastic wrap, and cool in the refrigerator for an hour or in the freezer for 30 minutes.

4. Ask an adult to help you preheat the oven to 350°F (175°C).

5. Place the chilled dough on a flat, lightly floured surface and roll out until it's about ¼ inch (6 mm) thick.

6. Cut the dough with your cookie cutters.

Step-by-Step:

7. Place the cookies 1 inch (2.5 cm) apart on the cookie sheet and bake in the preheated oven for 10–12 minutes, or until lightly browned. Take out to cool.

8. When the cookies are cool, they're ready to decorate!

Cupcake Menorah

The Hanukkah candlestick, known as the **menorah** or *hanukkiyah*, has eight branches plus one extra to hold the "shammash," or "helper candle" that lights the others. Menorahs come in all shapes and sizes, and they can even be edible! What better way to round off your Hanukkah celebrations than to light all nine candles on this cupcake menorah and then eat it for dessert!

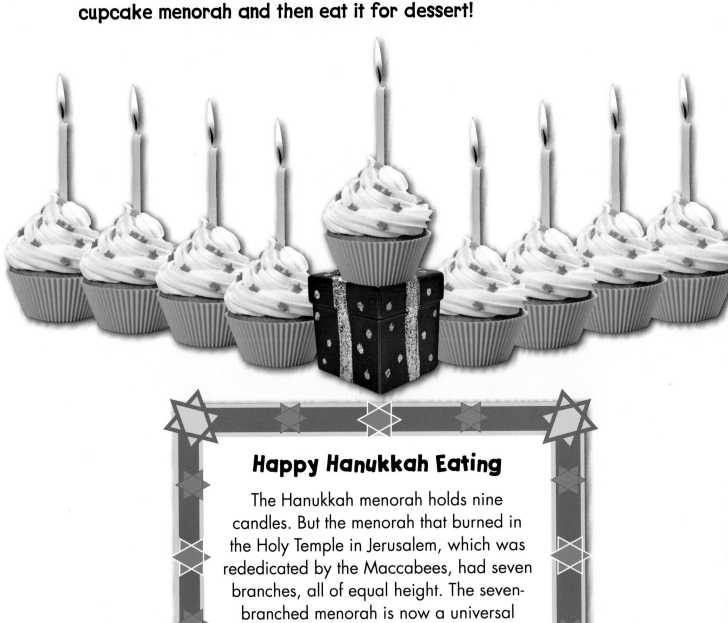

Happy Hanukkah Eating

The Hanukkah menorah holds nine candles. But the menorah that burned in the Holy Temple in Jerusalem, which was rededicated by the Maccabees, had seven branches, all of equal height. The seven-branched menorah is now a universal symbol of Judaism, displayed in many synagogues around the world.

You will need – ingredients:

These quantities will make about 10 to 12 cupcakes

1 cup sugar

½ cup butter, softened

2 eggs

2 teaspoons vanilla extract

1½ cups all-purpose flour

1¾ teaspoons baking powder

½ cup milk

Ready-made frosting in your favorite flavor

Sprinkles for decoration (if you wish)

You will need – equipment:

Cupcake pan

Cupcake wrappers

Large mixing bowl

Wooden spoon

Medium mixing bowl

Sieve for sifting flour

Electric hand mixer

Toothpick

Tray or platter

9 Hanukkah candles

Potholder or oven mitt for handling cupcake pan

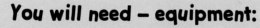

Remember to ask an adult for help when you are using the electric hand mixer and oven.

Step-by-Step:

1. Ask an adult to help you preheat the oven to 350°F (175°C).

2. Line the cupcake pan with the paper cupcake wrappers.

3. In the large mixing bowl, use the electric mixer to mix together the sugar and butter.

4. One at a time, beat the eggs into the sugar and butter mixture, then stir in the vanilla extract.

5. In the medium bowl, sift together the flour and baking powder.

6. Add the flour mixture to the creamy mixture and mix thoroughly.

7. Add the milk, stirring until the batter is smooth.

Step-by-Step:

8. Pour the batter into the paper cupcake wrappers so that each wrapper is about ⅔ full.

9. Bake for 20–25 minutes, until the cupcakes are light brown. Test to see if they're done by sticking a toothpick into the center of a cupcake. If it comes out clean, your cupcakes are ready to take out of the oven. Let the cupcakes cool.

10. To assemble your menorah, frost the cupcakes with the ready-made frosting, and add sprinkles to decorate if you wish.

11. Set out 9 cupcakes in a row on your tray or platter.

12. Raise the middle cupcake so that it's higher than the others to make the shammash. (Save any cupcakes that are left over, or share with a friend!)

13. Stick a candle in each cupcake. Your menorah is now ready to light and eat!

Glossary

dough (DOH) A thick mixture of flour and water, used for making such baked products as donuts, cookies, and bread.

Maccabees (MA-kuh-beez) From Hebrew for "hammer." A group of Jews who rebelled against the Syrian-Greeks in ancient Palestine (present-day Israel and neighboring region) more than 2,000 years ago.

menorah (meh-NOR-uh) A seven-branched or, for Hanukkah, an eight-branched candleholder that has become a well-known Jewish symbol.

miracle (MEER-uh-kul) An unexpected and favorable event that is not easily explained by science and that some may consider to be the work of a supreme being.

vitamin (VY-tuh-min) A substance found in foods that is needed by the body for health and growth.

Yiddish (YIH-dish) A language based in German, Hebrew, and Slavic languages and written in letters from the Hebrew alphabet. Used by Jews primarily in Central and Eastern Europe before World War II, it is also common in other parts of the world.

Index

Websites

For web resources related to the subject of this book,
go to: www.windmillbooks.com/weblinks
and select this book's title.